This Joyous Soul

BOOKS BY ALDEN SOLOVY

This Grateful Heart: Psalms and Prayers for a New Day
Jewish Prayers of Hope and Healing
Haggadah Companion: Meditations and Readings

This Joyous Soul

A New Voice for Ancient Yearnings

ALDEN SOLOVY

Foreword by Rabbi Sally J. Priesand

CENTRAL CONFERENCE OF AMERICAN RABBIS
New York · 2019/5779

In honor of my mother, Adrian A. Solovy

Library of Congress Cataloging-in-Publication Data

Names: Solovy, Alden T., 1957- author.
Title: This joyous soul : a new voice for ancient yearnings / Alden Solovy.
Description: New York : Central Conference of American Rabbis, [2019] |
    Includes bibliographical references and index.
Identifiers: LCCN 2018041308 (print) | LCCN 2018042381 (ebook) | ISBN
    9780881233322 | ISBN 9780881233315 (pbk. : alk. paper)
Subjects: LCSH: Judaism--Prayers and devotions. | Reform Judaism.
Classification: LCC BM665 (ebook) | LCC BM665 .S56 2018 (print) | DDC
    296.4/5046--dc23
LC record available at https://lccn.loc.gov/2018041308

Book interior designed and composed by Scott-Martin Kosofsky
at The Philidor Company, Rhinebeck, New York.

CCAR Press, 355 Lexington Avenue, New York, NY 10017
(212) 972-3636
www.ccarpress.org
Printed in U.S.A.
10 9 8 7 6 5 4 3 2 1

Contents

Amidah / Standing Prayers   59

Foreword

by Rabbi Sally J. Priesand

JUDAISM IS A LITURGICAL RELIGION. No matter what people believe about God, they find a role for prayer in their lives, as recorded in the Hebrew Bible regarding our ancestors. Abraham prayed for the well-being of Sodom and Gomorrah (Genesis 18:20–33). Jacob was the first to articulate an expression of awe when recognizing God's presence (Genesis 28:16–17). Moses asked God to heal his sister Miriam (Numbers 12:13). Hannah prayed for a child (I Samuel 1:8–15). Deborah sang a song of praise (Judges 5:1–3). The people Israel offered their first fruits as an act of worship (Deuteronomy 26:1–11). Aaron and his sons spoke the words of the Priestly Benediction (Numbers 6:23–27).

Similarly, in every generation, people pray to satisfy their need to draw near to something that is greater than themselves. Some use prayer as a means of expressing awe. Some recite prayers of thanksgiving as a way of recognizing blessings so often taken for granted. Others petition God in time of trouble, hoping for favor and mercy. Still others see prayer as a sermon to themselves, a reminder that we are partners with God in completing the world. We bear a responsibility to make real the words we pray.

Rabbi Menachem Mendel of Kotzk, also known as the Kotzker Rebbe, is remembered for his profoundly wise sayings, often simple, always insightful. When asked where God is, he answered that God dwells wherever people let God in.

Prayer is one of the ways in which we let God in, offering us the opportunity to open our hearts to God's presence. Thus, prayer books exist to help us communicate with God.

Prayer books enable us to look within to those values that shape our lives, and they assist us in gathering strength and courage for the tasks that remain undone. In many ways, a siddur is a history book that reflects the story of those who create it and those who pray from it. Each generation adds its own piece to the puzzle that is Judaism. A prayer book reflects those beliefs that are important to its users and provides insight into how Jewish tradition evolves from generation to generation.

Our children and grandchildren would probably find it strange to pray from a siddur that did not mention our Matriarchs, that talked about Israel only with the wish that the sacrificial cult be restored, and that consistently referred to God as "He." They are the product of their generation, and their response to a prayer book reflects the values with which they have grown up. A willingness to change makes possible the continuity of our tradition.

Alden Solovy is a worthy representative of our generation, for creating spiritually satisfying prayer. With *This Joyous Soul*, a companion volume to *This Grateful Heart*, he has artfully crafted once again a book of prayer that touches the soul in joyous ways. His ability to focus on the needs of the human heart makes prayer accessible to the individual and the community living in a contemporary world.

We begin our day by celebrating God as the Creator of life, a reminder that God creates through us and so makes us all creators too. Solovy has taken this God-given gift of creativity and developed it in such a way that our eyes are opened to new truths, our souls uplifted, and our spirits made tranquil. An extraordinarily gifted liturgist, he puts into perspective those things that matter most and challenges us to delve into the innermost recesses of our hearts, there to find God and understand that God cares who we are and how we act and what we do. Indeed, God depends on us, even as we depend on God.

This Joyous Soul was written to accompany *Mishkan T'filah*, with the hope that it would be placed in pew racks and used to enlarge the offerings found on the left-hand pages of the newest siddurim of the Reform Movement. That is good news, especially for those of us who attend synagogue services regularly and appreciate new material upon which to reflect. For those who do not attend quite as often, *This Joyous Soul* invites you to consider the ways in which prayer can enrich your life. Either way, these prayers are appropriate for communal prayer and/or individual reflection.

Our teacher Dr. Jakob Petuchowski, *z"l*, used to say that one generation's *kavanah* (intention) becomes the next generation's *keva* (fixed prayer). In other words, the private prayers of one generation become the public prayers of the next. I am confident that Alden Solovy's work will find a well-deserved place in whatever new prayer books are created by our generation, and for that I am eternally grateful.

Introduction

HAVE YOU EVER WISHED that your prayers could be like magic? I have. Say a prayer and heal my best friend. Poof. Say a prayer and save my wife from her depression and alcoholism. Poof. Say a prayer and rockets stop being shot at Israel. Peace and justice arrive for all. Not only Israel, the whole planet. Poof. It doesn't work that way. But you knew that.

Yet, we still pray for healing. We still pray for peace. We sing, we cry, we plead, we hope, we dream. We call out to God, knowing that prayers don't act like magic incantations. Prayer has a different sort of power.

Prayer isn't magic; it's alchemy. Prayer is a practice that will change me, change you, and change those around us. Prayer is discovery. Prayer gives voice to our deepest desires. Prayer is transformative. It impacts realms beyond our understanding. Deep inside the act of prayer is the yearning to be witnessed by the Witness, to receive blessings from the Source, to gain comfort from the Well, to gain strength from the Rock, to find wholeness in the One.

To pray is a bold, perhaps brazen spiritual act. Nothing short of sheer audacity. To pray is to have faith that our words have an impact on worlds, the world of heaven and the world of earth. To pray is to declare that our words can ascend to reach divine realms and that they will be heard. To pray is to suggest that God desires our prayers, perhaps even needs them.

We participate in this remarkably daring and courageous

act because we believe prayer matters. Even when that faith is shaken, we yearn to believe that our prayers make a difference. We go so far as to pray for our prayers to be heard. We dare to pray on behalf of our prayers.

Prayer is audacious because, in the process, we must assume that our voices are heard in holy realms. We have standing at the gates of heaven. We are familiar to the divine consciousness. We can call on God's holy name.

This is spiritual bravery: to have faith in a power that operates beyond our basic senses, to have faith that a unique force is created when the energy of human words and emotions is articulated in combination with the intention of reaching out to the Divine.

When we pray as Jews, we turn first to our siddur, our prayer book, the collected liturgy of millennia. The siddur is layered with the dreams and aspirations of our ancestors. It's a catalogue of our history and a recitation of our theology. It isn't a book. It is a set of books that has evolved over hundreds of years, influenced by both time and location. The result is another paradox. There is no one single siddur used by all the Jewish people, but there are common prayers and rhythms among all our prayer traditions. And while the siddurim that have been handed down for generations can be enchanting, the prayers can feel obscure and foreign.

The contrast is startling. To pray is brave. To pray from a siddur, however, is an act of surrender. We surrender to the words of the authors—the text as presented by redactors, editors, and translators—whether using a traditional volume or a more modern, liberal text. To pray from a siddur is to accept the theological and liturgical choices of rabbis, scholars, and teachers. These are leaders who know the historical, spiritual, and scriptural underpinnings of our prayers. These are scholars best suited to create a prayer book that will have continuity with the past and a resonance in the present.

We need to engage with a siddur that offers continuity with our past and with the breadth of Jewish communities of the present, as well as the freedom to pray in a more modern voice consistent with our generation's understanding of Jewish spirituality. *This Joyous Soul: A New Voice for Ancient Yearnings* provides a modern expression to classic prayers as handed down for millennia and redacted by the rabbis and scholars of modern times. It is organized around the weekday morning service. Although it can be used with any prayer book, it is structured around *Mishkan T'filah*, with many of the section heads matching those of that volume.

This is a book of "left-hand" pages. Those of you who use *Mishkan T'filah* and *Mishkan HaNefesh*—as well as a variety of other prayer books published in the United States and elsewhere—are familiar with the idea. For the core sections of prayers in these volumes, you'll find that the Hebrew and a faithful translation of prayers appear on the right-hand pages. The left-hand pages offer alternatives: poetry, meditations, interpretations, challenges, reframes, and flights of fancy based on the prayer on the right. These left-hand pages give individuals additional doorways into personal contemplation and understanding, while providing congregations and their clergy the opportunity to use new texts to create layers of meaning in communal worship or to respond to the immediate issues of the day.

Many of the themes of the weekday morning service recur in both the afternoon and evening services, as well as Shabbat and holiday services. Thus, this volume provides a versatile tool for both individuals and congregations. My hope is that congregations will place copies of *This Joyous Soul* alongside their regular siddur—in the pews or on the rack of prayer books—as a supplement to worship or for congregants to use in moments of silent contemplation. Prayers specific to Shabbat and the holy days can also be found in the companion volume *This Grateful Heart: Psalms and Prayers for a New Day*; congregations and individuals might consider using these two volumes together.

This Joyous Soul also has a place in the home. It offers a doorway into classic daily prayer, with nontraditional pieces that can be a supplement, or perhaps a starting place, for a personal prayer practice.

My hope is that this book will open new doorways into your personal prayer life. I hope that it serves as an invitation to explore the siddur with fresh eyes, that it opens your curiosity about the themes and intentions handed down for generations. Deeper still, I hope that *This Joyous Soul* becomes a source of inspiration for you to write your own prayers, for you to express your own voice of spiritual alchemy. Let *This Joyous Soul* feed your soul with the love of prayer. May the words of your heart lift you, shine within you, and bring you joy, comfort, and peace.

Acknowledgements

God of creativity,
Bless those who have supported me,
Helped and encouraged me,
Sharing their wisdom and talents
As I pursue the call to write
In service to Your holy name.
You have sent teachers and counselors,
Friends and guides,
Writers and musicians,
Provocateurs and cheerleaders,
From all streams of Judaism
And from a myriad of faiths,
Of all genders and identities,
To travel together on this journey of prayer and blessing.
May their enthusiasm return to them, tenfold, as gifts
*   in their lives*
And in the lives of those whom they love.
May their wisdom continue to echo into the world
Yielding holiness and love in the light of their presence.
Bless them, sustain them, and grant them
Health and happiness,
Joy and peace.
Amen.

THIS JOYOUS SOUL represents an evolution of my work, the next step on a journey to help create meaningful doorways into a life of prayer. That evolution would not be possible without the people who have become part of a community who have encouraged my work. Thanks to all of you who've supported me by reading, sharing, and commenting on my prayers and poetry online. Seeing my readership grow is a source of great joy.

I'm blessed by the love, dedication, inspiration, insights, and faith of more people than I can count. Chief among them, my family has been a constant source of encouragement. To my daughters, my mother, and my sisters, a thank you that only you can understand. I continue to be blessed by the memory of my wife, Ami *z"l*, who believed in my writing long before I ever did.

The evolution of my writing has been blessed by a wide variety of individuals who've not only offered advice on my work and topics for new prayers, but challenged me to explore a broad set of topics—Talmud, new Jewish music, classic *piyutim*, visual arts, the theology of prayer, academic articles on the siddur, the history of core *t'filot*—to deepen my connection with both the heart and mind of prayer. Some have inspired me with their own teaching and writing. The list is lovely and long. Here I focus on the people who have had an impact on this volume: Rabbi Ruth Abusch-Magder, Asher Arbit, Anita Diamant, Rabba Yaffa Epstein, Cantor Erin Frankel, Michael Haruni, Rabbi Sharyn Henry, Rabbi Paul Kipnes, Rabbi Peter Knobel, Michael B. Miller, Peta Jones Pellach, and Randall Williams. My apologies to anyone whom I might have missed.

Three extraordinary individuals whom I'm blessed to call friends read the manuscript and provided heartfelt words of support. Special thanks to Rabbi Denise Eger, Cantor Evan Kent, and Rabbi Leon Morris for your generous endorsements.

Rabbi Sally J. Priesand's introduction is rich in Torah and richer in insight about the human impulse to pray and drive to make prayers our own. Rabbi, I'm stunned by the bounty of your praise for this book. It's an honor to have our names appear together on the cover.

A word of deep thanks to those who had a direct hand in creating *This Joyous Soul*. First, thanks to the CCAR Press Council committee for supporting this project; in particular, Rabbi Donald Goor, who chaired the committee and has been a steadfast supporter of my work. Thanks to Debra Corman for copyediting, Michele Kwitkin for proofreading, and Scott-Martin Kosofsky for design and compositing.

The professional team at CCAR Press is skilled, dedicated, energetic, caring, and a pleasure to work with. Thank you, Carly Linden, Deborah Smilow, and Rabbi Dan Medwin. Two CCAR team members have been second to none in their creativity, enthusiasm, and constant support for marketing and promoting both *This Joyous Soul* and the predecessor volume, *This Grateful Heart*. Thank you, Ortal Bensky and Sasha Smith. Thanks to Rabbi Steven Fox, outgoing CCAR chief executive, for supporting both of these books. I've been blessed to work with essentially the same skilled and enthusiastic CCAR Press team on both volumes.

My deepest thanks to Rabbi Hara Person. Hara, you have a passion for books and a passion for prayer that makes working with you an act of art, an act of love, and an act of blessing. I'm thrilled that the cover photo is one of yours. The fact that you were snapping gorgeous sunsets just as we were looking at cover designs is no accident. It beautifully suggests the story of a joyous soul seeking God. You've been a steadfast friend—a coach, a consultant, an editor, and advocate—while never losing sight of the needs of the reader, the Reform Movement, our rabbis, and the hearts of all who love and need to pray. You bless me. You bless us all.

Birchot HaShachar
Morning Blessings

Modeh/Modah Ani

מוֹדֶה\וּמוֹדָה אֲנִי לְפָנֶיךָ,
מֶלֶךְ חַי וְקַיָּם,
שֶׁהֶחֱזַרְתָּ בִּי נִשְׁמָתִי בְּחֶמְלָה,
רַבָּה אֱמוּנָתֶךָ.

Modeh/modah ani l'fanecha,
Melech chai v'kayam,
she-hechezarta bi nishmati b'chemlah,
rabbah emunatecha.

I thank You, God,
Creator of life, Eternal One,
For restoring my soul to me with love
Filled with Your eternal trust.

I thank You, God,
Creator of life, Eternal One,
For restoring my love with trust
Filled with Your eternal hope.

I thank You, God,
Creator of life, Eternal One,
For restoring my trust with hope
Filled with Your eternal kindness.

I thank You, God,
Creator of life, Eternal One,
For restoring my hope with kindness
Filled with Your eternal justice.

I thank You, God,
Creator of life, Eternal One,
For restoring my kindness with justice
Filled with Your eternal mercy.

I thank You, God,
Creator of life, Eternal One,
For restoring my justice with mercy
Filled with Your eternal peace.

I thank You, God,
Creator of life, Eternal One,
For restoring my mercy with peace
Filled with Your eternal soul.

I thank You, God,
Creator of life, Eternal One,
For restoring my peace with soul
Filled with Your eternal love.

I thank You, God,
Creator of life, Eternal One,
For restoring my soul with love
Filled with Your eternal trust.

First Bird

The first bird of morning
Sings alone,
For the joy of breathing,
For the glory of seeing,
For the love of being,
Alive and awake
In this world.

The second bird of morning
Sings a duet
In the gentle breeze,
As daybreak meets the earth
With the wonder of being
Alive and awake
In this world.

Then the chorus appears.
The pitch rises.
Still, they make space
For solos and for silence.
They make space
To hear.
They make space
To rejoice in being
Alive and awake
In this world.

Wrap and Bind

With a sheet of broad cloth
We wrap ourselves
In the unreachable.
Fringes tied with turns and knots.
We wrap ourselves
In God's holy shelter.

With each turn of the strap,
Black leather strung from a box,
We bind ourselves
To the unknowable.
We bind ourselves
To God's Holy Word.

How do we hold onto the gifts around us?
How do we see the mysteries near to us?

Wrap and bind.
Wrap and bind.
Throughout our lives,
Wrap and bind.

Your Dwelling Place

When I pray,
When I quiet my mind and open my heart,
I become a servant
In the house of God.

God,
I love Your house,
Your habitation,
The dwelling place of Your glory.
Let me serve You with my hands,
With the toil of healing the world,
With the labor of kindness and compassion.
And I will become Your abode
Of love and charity,
Of thanksgiving and peace,
Doing Your will in joy,
Rejoicing in Your work.
How goodly are thy tents, O Jacob,
Thy dwellings, O Israel!

Let my life become a temple,
A sanctuary of praise and service,
And You will dwell
In me.

Entrances and Exits

This moment is an entrance:
An entrance to your breath,
An entrance to your heart,
An entrance to your journey,
An entrance to your destination.

This moment is an exit:
An exit from your solitude,
An exit from your fear,
An exit from your wounds,
An exit from your cage.

God of Old,
Open our eyes to the majesty
That surrounds us.
Grant us the courage
To enter this day
With wonder and amazement,
With enthusiasm and joy,
With strength and with hope.
Teach us to dance
Toward holiness.
Teach us to sail
Toward beauty.
Teach us to love
In the direction of wholeness and peace.

The world is Yours
In fullness and glory,
Given to us as a gift
So that we may rejoice
In the mysteries
Around us.

Let God

Let God
Hold majesty before your eyes
And mystery before your heart.

Let God
Place strength in your hands
And radiance in your soul.

Let God
Lead you to awe and wonder
And redeem you from fear and shame.

You are cloud and horizon,
A bird in solo flight,
Seeking your flock,
Seeking your journey,
Seeking your place.

Let God
Place healing in your hours
And rejoicing in all of your days.

Let God
Find you in the open sky
And lift you in joy and grace.

Being Present

God, help me live this day
In a way that draws Your favor,
That summons Your gifts and Your blessings,
That attracts holiness and light.

Give me courage and strength,
Hope and understanding.

Help me to be present in my life.
Help me to be present in my day.
Help me to be present for others.
Help me to be present for myself.

Let me live awake and aware,
Vital and energetic,
Casting off the chains of doubt and fear.

God of hidden worlds,
God of secret realms,
God of trial and triumph,
You have given me moments and choices,
Hours and opportunities,
Days to build
And days to renew.
Let me live this day with wisdom,
Awake to moments for healing,
Dedicating my hands and my heart
To the work of creation.

And Your gifts will appear quietly,
Gently,
Sweet like morning dew
To refresh my heart.

Receiving Blessings

Ancient One,
Open my heart to receive
The blessings around me,
Kindness and wisdom,
Friendship and understanding,
Tenderness and compassion,
Moments of holiness,
Messages from heaven.

Source and Shelter,
Open my heart to bless others
With the fullness of my being,
With joy and thanksgiving,
From a hope for healing
And a pulse of love,
To fill the world with benedictions.

Rock and Redeemer,
Open my heart to welcome
The blessings around me,
A fountain of grace
To fill my soul
With gratitude and courage,
With wonder and peace.

Prayer for You, Prayer for Me

What brilliance is this?
What divine secret of blessing,
That my prayer for you
Is a prayer for me?

Can love be so simple
Or holiness so close,
Can joy be as near
Or awe and wonder as ready
To blossom in the glow of faith?

May you know peace.
May you know health and healing.
May you know hope.
May you know laughter and delight.

What majestic gift,
God of Old,
Have You hidden
Inside our prayers,
That my prayers for others
Resound with joy
And echo in my being?

Ancient One,
Master of Blessings,
Who calls upon us
To summon
The light of holiness
Into the world with our prayers.

Sacred Silly

Wouldn't it be fun,
Just one time,
To secretly slip a goofy prayer
Inside the siddur,
Say, in the middle of the *Amidah*,
Where an unsuspecting Yid
Like you or me
Might just crack up
In sacred silliness,
Holy happiness,
Loving laughter,
As a testimony
To the juicy joy
Of Jewish jubilation?

So serious
These liturgists,
These poets and *paytanim*.
Let's g'faw for God.
Let's laugh out loud in praise.
Let's giggle in thanksgiving.

עִבְדוּ אֶת יי בְּשִׂמְחָה, בְּאוּ לְפָנָיו בִּרְנָנָה.
Ivdu et Adonai b'simchah, bo-u l'fanav birnanah.
Worship Adonai with gladness,
Come into God's presence with singing.

Let joy rise up to the gates of prayer.
Let laughter shake the highest heavens.

Each Day

To start this day with joy.
To end this day with peace.
To start this day with longing.
To end this day released.

Live each day with valor,
With trust, with hope, with faith.
Live each day with wonder,
With kindness, awe, and grace.

Hold fast to sacred moments.
Hold fast to precious love.
Hold fast to one another.
Hold fast to God above.

Hold courage through the hours,
And humor through the tears.
Hold God above your sorrows.
Hold God above your fears.

To You I must surrender,
O God of hidden spheres.
You are Source and Shelter.
To You I pledge my years.

Morning Blessings

Blessed are You, Adonai our God,
Sovereign of the universe . . .

    . . . Who created a world of luminous wonder.
    . . . Who created a world of radiant splendor.
    . . . Who created a world of shimmering glory.
    . . . Source of life and health.
    . . . Well of joy and love.
    . . . Fountain of forgiveness and hope.
    . . . Who grants rest and renewal.
    . . . Who grants strength and fortitude.
    . . . Who grants wisdom and understanding.
    . . . Who delights in prayer.
    . . . Who delights in service.
    . . . Who delights in righteousness.

Blessed are You, Adonai our God,
Sovereign of the universe,
Creator of this new day, Source of sustenance,
Bless the works of my hands so that I become
A source of holiness and healing.

God's Morning

Calm or wind.
Cloud or sun.
Warm or cool.
It's God's morning.
A gift.
A promise.
A bird gliding on a breeze,
Singing ancient songs,
That need no translation.
A ray of secret light
Stored for this very moment
Since the beginning of time.

Let us rejoice.
Let us sing.
Let us tremble with love,
While the Artist paints
The sky and the hills,
The seas and the plains,
In the colors of majesty.

It's God's morning.
Sent as a reminder
To love and to hope.
Sent as a reminder
To celebrate
The glory of Creation.

Before Studying Torah

Our Torah,
God's Torah,
This *eitz chayim*,
This tree of life
That has sustained us
For millennia,
Must be replanted
In every generation.
Taught, tended, loved,
Cultivated deep in the fertile
Soil of our souls,
So that righteousness and mercy
Will take root in our hearts
And bear fruit in our deeds.

God of wisdom,
Source of wonder,
Let my teaching today
Become another seed of Your word,
Bearing blessings for Your people,
Bringing light into the world,
In service to Your holy name.

בָּרוּךְ אַתָּה יי אֱלֹהֵינוּ מֶלֶךְ הָעוֹלָם,
אֲשֶׁר קִדְּשָׁנוּ בְּמִצְוֹתָיו וְצִוָּנוּ
לַעֲסוֹק בְּדִבְרֵי תוֹרָה.

Baruch atah, Adonai Eloheinu, Melech haolam,
asher kid'shanu b'mitzvotav v'tzivanu
laasok b'divrei Torah.

Blessed are You, Adonai our God,
Sovereign of the universe, who hallows us
with mitzvot, commanding us
to engage with words of Torah.

Meditation on Mitzvot

It's simple, really,
This list of things we do,
As a people,
This list of things I do,
To live in a good way,
For others and myself,
To leave a legacy of love,
To leave the world
Just a little better each day.

A kind word.
A gentle hand.
A loving voice.
A giving heart.

It's not so simple, really,
To remember to live this way.
Always.
So we arrive early to study Torah
And strive for devotion in prayer,
To remember to honor all beings
With compassion and understanding,
Living a life of mitzvot in joy and service,
So that Torah will resound from our hearts,
Through our words and deeds,
Into the world,
And into the generations to come.

P'sukei D'zimrah

Morning Psalms

Blessed Name

Blessed is the broken heart
That yearns to heal in the warmth of love.
Blessed is the wounded soul
That yearns to heal in the whisper of hope.
Blessed is the aching spirit
That yearns to heal in the mystery of eternity.
Blessed are the darkened eyes
That learn to see in the river of light.
Blessed is the shallow breath
That learns to expand in the heartbeat of Creation.
Blessed are the silenced ears
That learn to hear in the whisper of the wind.

Blessed is this journey.
Blessed is this prayer.
Blessed is your heart.

Source of all,
The One who creates,
The One who sustains,
The One who comforts and guides,
The One who spoke and the world came to be,
Blessed is Your name.

Light of God

How bright Your garment of light!
How vast the curtain of heaven!
How great Your splendor and majesty!

I stand before You
In service to Torah and mitzvot.
Ready. Willing. Present.
Dedicating my heart to You.
My soul singing in praise.

In Your light, we see light.
In Your light, we are bathed in light.
Wrapped in Your light,
We are sheltered by light.

Blessed are You,
Bringing light to the upright in heart.

The Gifts of Our Lives

With gratitude and appreciation
We give thanks for the gifts
That flow into our lives day by day,
A river of divine blessing.

For You are the well of Abundance,
The source of Beauty,
A foundation of Courage,
And the crown of Dreams.

You are the well of Energy,
The source of Faith,
A foundation of Grace,
And the crown of Hope.

You are the well of Insight,
The source of Justice,
A foundation of Kindness,
And the crown of Love.

You are the well of Mercy,
The source of Nourishment,
The fountain of Our Lives,
And the crown of Peace.

You are the well of Quiet,
The source of Righteousness,
A foundation of Strength,
And the crown of Truth.

For You are the well of Understanding,
The source of Vitality,
A foundation of Wonder,
And the crown of Years.

With gratitude and appreciation
We give thanks for the gifts
That flow into our lives day by day,
A river of divine blessing.

Hiding My Face

What does it mean
When I hide my face from You?
When I withhold my prayers,
My voice, my song?

Your Glory is like the sun,
Warming my skin and the land.
I am afraid that You will
Take all of me,
Leaving me parched and burned,
Unrecognizable.

You who stand thirsty at God's well,
You cannot run from your sacred calling,
You cannot run from God's voice.
Ignore it perhaps,
Postpone it perhaps,
Until the weight of your destiny
Swallows you whole
And there is nowhere left to hide.

אַשְׁרֵי יוֹשְׁבֵי בֵיתֶךָ
Ashrei yoshvei veitecha,
Happy are those who dwell in Your house.
Happy are those who sing Your praise.
Happy are those who do Your works.
Happy are those who answer Your call.

Open my hands,
Open my heart,
Draw me close to You.
Guard me. Guide me. Save me.

תְּהִלַּת יי יְדַבֶּר־פִּי,

T'hilat Adonai y'daber pi,
My mouth shall utter the praise of Adonai,

וִיבָרֵךְ כָּל־בָּשָׂר שֵׁם קָדְשׁוֹ לְעוֹלָם וָעֶד.

Viy'vareich kol basar sheim kodsho l'olam va-ed.
And all creatures shall bless God's holy name forever and ever.

In Gratitude for Your Gifts

Guardian of my life.
Guide of my spirit:
>In Awe we seek You,
>With Blessings we reach You,
>In Communion we call to You,
>With Devotion we come to You.
>With Enthusiasm we turn to You,
>In Faith we trust in You,
>With Gratitude we look to You,
>In Humility we yearn for You,
>With Inspiration we return to You,
>In Joy we praise You.

Source of all being,
Light of the earth:
>In Kindness You heal us,
>In Love You sustain us,
>In Mercy You forgive us,
>With Nobility You bless us,
>With Openness You hear us,
>With Peace You comfort us.
>In Quiet we hear You,
>With Radiance You bestow divine gifts,
>With Splendor You renew the world,
>In Trust You've given us free will.

Soul of the universe,
Grant us:
>Understanding to follow Your word,
>Vigor to live by Your law,
>Wisdom to follow Your path,
>Yearning to study Torah,
>Zeal for justice and peace.

Sing Out

When you feel the light of holiness,
The radiance of love,
The shimmering of glory,
The luminous glow of spirit . . .

When you inhale wonder
And exhale awe . . .

When mystery and majesty flow
Through your pulsing veins . . .

When God's whisper becomes a thundering
Blast of the shofar . . .

When your soul remembers its
Place in the heavens . . .

Sing out!
Sing out your joy.
Sing out your praise.

When you feel the light of Torah,
The radiance of mitzvot,
The shimmering of prayer,
The luminous glow of loving-kindness . . .

Sing out!
Sing out to God.
Your voice will join the chorus of angels
And your heart will know
The secret of eternity.

Sing Praises

Quiet now.
Breathe.
Breathe and listen.

Listen to the prayers in the wind.
Listen to the joy on the breeze.
Listen to the hope in the heavens.
For love and life are yours.
Holiness and power remain.
Wonder and awe
Shimmer from sunset to sunset.

This is the moment where love meets joy,
Where hope meets surrender.

What is that music?
What is that radiance?
What is that yearning?

Quiet now.
Breathe.
Breathe and listen.
Listen to your own voice.
Listen to your own prayers.

This is your power and your peace.
This is your pulse and your heartbeat.
This is your life.
Sing praises,
Sing praises.

Place Your Name upon Us

Place Your name upon us,
God of grace,
So that we may bring peace and love
Into the world.

Place Your name upon us,
God of justice,
So that we may bring awe and discipline
Into the world.

Place Your name upon us,
God of beauty,
So that we may bring harmony and compassion
Into the world.

Place Your name upon us,
God of eternity,
So that we may bring strength and endurance
Into the world.

Place Your name upon us,
God of splendor,
So that we may bring humility and wonder
Into the world.

Place Your name upon us,
God the foundation,
So that we may bring healing and bonding
Into the world.

Place Your name upon us,
God of sovereignty,
So that we may bring nobility and majesty
Into the world.

Place Your name upon us,
God of wisdom,
So that we may bring righteousness and Torah
Into the world.

Place Your name upon us,
God of understanding,
So that we may bring mystery and creation
Into the world.

Place Your name upon us,
God the One,
So that we may return to You
Our Source, the Crown, our destination.

In Praise

Hallelujah at sunset.
Hallelujah at daybreak.
Hallelujah at dusk.
Hallelujah at dawn.
Hallelujah with pauper and prince,
With beggar and king.
Hallelujah with all God's works.

This is my prayer, God of Sarah,
To declare Your glory in all things.

Hallelujah in sunshine,
Hallelujah in shadow.
Hallelujah in calm.
Hallelujah in storm.
Hallelujah in peace.
Hallelujah at war.
Hallelujah in shelter.
Hallelujah when all comfort and protection
Appear lost.

This is our prayer, God of Abraham,
To praise You every moment.
To praise You,
To sing to You,
To dance for You,
To declare Hallelujah with our lives.

Sing Hallelujah

Hallelujah
A hymn of glory,
A chant of praise,
A song of thanksgiving.
Voices raised, hearts to heaven.
Lungs full and strong.
A breath, a note, a lyric, a tune.
A call of love,
An echo of truth,
Resounding with joy and praise.

Let my hopes carry me toward wondrous deeds.
Let my heart guide me toward sacred wisdom.
Let my breath lead me to majestic truth.
Let my words exalt Your holy name.

Hallelujah
A song of hope,
A harmony of justice,
A chorus of mercy.

God of Miriam,
Prophet who danced by the sea,
Teach me the song of life,
Of dedication and zeal,
Of wonder and glory.
Teach me to sing my Hallelujah.
Teach me to live my Hallelujah.
A song of righteousness.
A song of thanksgiving.
A song for the generations.

Dance Hallelujah

Hallelujah
A dance of wonder,
A dance of joy and thanksgiving.
Arms raised, hands to the sky.
Feet solid, connected to earth.
A step, a bend, a twirl, a leap.
A breath of light,
A stream of color,
Spinning toward radiance and splendor.

Let my feet lead me toward Your holy realm.
Let my legs carry me toward Your divine word.
Let my arms lift praises toward Your marvelous works.
Let my body exclaim the power of Your awesome ways.

Hallelujah
A dance of light and love,
A dance of energy and endurance,
A dance of humility and grace.

God of Miriam,
Prophet who danced by the sea,
Teach me the dance of awe and mystery,
Of devotion and ecstasy,
Of passion and praise.
Teach me to dance my Hallelujah.
Teach me to live my Hallelujah.
A dance of radiance,
A dance of splendor,
A dance of peace.

The Details of Beauty

Remember
The details of beauty
With your eyes.
The autumn leaf,
A baby's cry,
Small wonders to remind you
Of joy and wonder.

Remember
The details of love
With your breath.
The soft smile
And gentle hand,
Small wonders to remind you
Of awe and majesty.

Remember
The details of faith
With your pulse,
The quiet prayer,
The hymn of glory,
Small wonders to remind you
Of devotion and service.

God of Old,
The details of beauty
Surround us.
Love and faith are
Our inheritance.
Teach us to see clearly in each day
The small wonders
You set before us.
To take them in,
To feel their power
And to rejoice.

The Rhythm of Wonder

When the mountains sing,
When the seas dance,
When a crescent moon glides through the heavens
And the sun lifts day from night,
When the rivers waltz to hymns of rain
And the oceans drum on cliffs of stone,
When the caper bush wakes
And the wild iris blooms,
Remember this,
It's not the wind that lifts the eagle.
The eagle lifts the wind.

You are the love
That frees the baritone hills
And the pirouette skies,
A shaft of light to loose the crescendos of glory
And the colors of awe,
A heartbeat summoning the rhythm of wonder,
A yearning to hear the pulse of God.

When silence resounds with music,
When darkness radiates light,
When Creation reaches up
From the core of the earth,
And eternity is a breeze
From the edge of the universe,
When the call to holiness shines brilliant
In the breathless dawn,
Remember this,
It's not the prayer that lifts the blessing.
The blessing lifts the prayer.

Sacred Cargo

You carry sacred cargo within
Your *ruach*, your *nefesh*, your *n'shamah*,
The spirit and breath of holiness,
Given to you by the One,
The Source,
HaKadosh Baruch Hu,
Blessed be God's holy name.

You carry sacred cargo within
Your heart, your lungs, your blood,
The vitality of holiness,
Given to you by the One,
The Source,
HaKadosh Baruch Hu,
Blessed be God's holy name.

You carry sacred cargo within
Your hands, your voice, your strength,
The instruments of holiness,
Given to you by the One,
The Source,
HaKadosh Baruch Hu,
Blessed be God's holy name.

Sh'ma
and Related Blessings

❦

This Moment

How did I arrive in this place?
This joy and wonder.
This grief and loss.
This hour. This moment. This life.
Choices. Events. God.
My decisions. The decisions of others.
The hand of our Creator.

Holy One,
Help me to see that I am exactly
Where I need to be
To learn and to serve,
To be and to become,
To live as an instrument of healing and love,
Charity and forgiveness,
Kindness and grace.

How did I arrive in this moment?
How did I get this blessing,
This gift,
To be exactly where I can learn and serve
In God's holy name?

Finding God

Finding God is
As simple as
Breathing in
The morning air,
As simple as
Seeing
The light
Around you,
As simple as
Feeling
Your heartbeat
Fill your chest.

Learning to breathe, to see, to feel
The presence of holiness . . .
That is the secret.
That is the journey.
How quiet and still,
How open and aware,
How ready and willing must we be
To see the
Extraordinary
In the mundane?
Before we can see a
Bush in flames
That is not consumed?
Before we take off our shoes
In the light of awe and majesty?

Finding God is
As simple as
Breathing in mystery,
As simple as
Seeing the radiance around you,
As simple as
Feeling glory fill your limbs,
And wonder fill your chest.

This Is the Place

This is the place where the beginning and the
    ending meet,
Where the vast sky greets the firmament of heaven,
Where the finite and the infinite touch,
Where the breathing in becomes the breathing out.

This is the place where darkness meets the light,
Where mourning surrenders to rejoicing,
Where what we are summons what we may become,
Where all hearts beat together in joy.

Oh to see so clearly.
Oh to live so gently.
Oh to be so simply.
Oh to love so sweetly.

This is the place where holiness can be held,
Where mystery shimmers and eternity shines,
Where the core of the earth burns with the fire
    of starlight,
Where majesty rises like the sun
In radiant brilliant luminous wonder.

About Miracles

Majestic Sovereign,
Source of awe and wonder,
When did You decide
To make miracles so simple,
So gentle, so quiet, and so small?
Did our fear of Your voice
Echoing from the mountaintop
Push You away?
Or was this Your plan all along,
To show us Your glory
In fire and smoke,
In the parted sea,
In the darkness and in the light,
And then to draw away
So that we would
Yearn for You to be near,
So that we would yearn
For Your power and might,
For Your holiness,
And for Your salvation?
Or are You waiting, patiently,
To return, again, with signs
And wonders?

For Creation

Author of life,
Architect of Creation,
Artist of earth,
Your works declare Your holy name.

Mighty rivers,
Turbulent seas,
Towering mountains,
Rolling hills,
Vast spaces of brilliance and grandeur.

You created palette and paint,
Color and hue,
Shape and form,
Abundant and beautiful,
Glorious and majestic,
Full of mystery and wonder.

Blessed are You,
With divine love You created a world of splendor.

This Joyous Soul

God's love lingers
Where the rainbows hide,
Waiting to burst forth
In radiant glory.

How this joyous soul yearns for You!
Your blessings and Your grace,
Your wisdom and Your compassion,
This joyous voice sings Your praises.

God's love lingers
At the gates of your heart,
Waiting to burst forth
In luminous splendor.

Gravity and Light

Torah is gravity,
Binding us to our ancestors,
Holding us near to our God,
Anchoring us with wisdom and understanding.
Torah is gravity,
Tying our lives
To our history and our destiny.

Mitzvot are light,
Illuminating our path,
Brightening our days,
Showing us the way to holiness and service,
Leading us to heal the world.
Mitzvot are light,
Shining around us,
With beauty.

Torah is gravity.
May your feet never falter.
Mitzvot are light.
May your hands shine with grace.

Gravity and light surround us.
Torah and mitzvot enliven us.
Blessed are God's gifts.

For Prayer

Source of all,
Fill my heart with joy and thanksgiving,
My eyes with vision and hope,
My limbs with strength and vigor.
Fill my breath with kindness and grace,
So that the wonder of Your blessings never leaves me.
Then my lips will remember to sing in holy praise,
To sing of beauty and glory and love.

Rock of Israel,
We pray for the gift of prayer,
For song and music,
For silence and devotion,
For steadfast love of You.

With prayer we bless You.
With song we praise You.
With music we extol You.
With silence we hear You.
With devotion we follow You.
In love we declare Your holy name.

Gathering: A Dream of Reunion

וַהֲבִיאֵנוּ לְשָׁלוֹם מֵאַרְבַּע כַּנְפוֹת הָאָרֶץ
וְתוֹלִיכֵנוּ קוֹמְמִיּוּת לְאַרְצֵנוּ...

Vahavi-einu l'shalom mei-arba kanfot haaretz
V'tolicheinu kom'miyut l'artzeinu ...

Gather us in peace from the four corners of the earth
And lead us upright to our land ...

FIRST TZITZIT: Gathering Fringes
With the first knotted string in hand,
I imagine the journey home,
Home to the land of our mothers and fathers,
Holy and full of promise, labor and love,
To build a life of wonder and awe.
This is me.
This is my pilgrimage to sacred soil.
This is my dream of holiness and redemption.
I am the first tzitzit,
Returning home.

SECOND TZITZIT: Gathering Hearts
The second fraying string in hand,
I imagine my children, my family, my household
Returning with me to our homeland
To build and to renew our ancestral blood.
This is my family.
This is our journey to hallowed ground.
This is our wholeness and rebirth.
We are the second tzitzit,
Returning home.

THIRD TZITZIT: Gathering Moments
The third worn string in hand,
I imagine you, my community, my *kahal*,
Returning together to our Source and Shelter,
To consecrate the ancient land and our holy vow.
This is my village.
This is our journey to mystery and majesty.
This is our bond of ages.
We are the third tzitzit,
Returning home.

FINAL TZITZIT: Gathering Millennia
The final woolen string in hand,
I imagine all of us, from all corners of the earth,
Returning with songs of praise and rejoicing,
To claim our place among the nation of Israel.
This is my people.
This is our journey of destiny.
This is our covenant.
We are the final tzitzit, separate no more,
Returning home.

Affirmation of Faith

Hear, O Israel,
> The covenant we made
> Together on Sinai
> Is a pledge for all time,
> A vow for the ages,
> To do and to listen,
> To teach and to learn
> With the fullness of our hearts,
> From the depths of our souls
> And the strength of our being,
> Binding ourselves to

Adonai our God
> With Torah and mitzvot,
> Binding our lives to each other
> With righteousness and charity,
> So that blessings will rain down from heaven
> To feed our hearts and fill our land
> With God's abundant gifts,
> The brilliance and wonder
> That flow from service to God's Holy Word,
> In remembrance of Creation
> And our liberation from slavery,
> Declaring throughout the generations:

God is One,
> God is One,
> God is One.

שְׁמַע יִשְׂרָאֵל יי אֱלֹהֵינוּ יי אֶחָד!

Sh'ma Yisrael, Adonai Eloheinu, Adonai Echad!
Hear, O Israel, Adonai is our God, Adonai is One!

Who Is Like You

Who is like You,
God of mystery and majesty,
Distant and present,
Thundering and quiet,
The beginning and the end,
The atom and the cosmos,
The darkness and the light,
The One and the All,
Pillar and foundation,
Artist of sea and sky,
Author of the miraculous and the mundane,
Source of life,
Blessing and sustaining Creation.

Who is like You,
Glorious in holiness,
To whom we praise,
To whom we give thanks,
The God who redeemed us from Egypt,
The God who parted the sea,
The God to whom Miriam and Moses
Led us in song.

Miriam's Word

Listen, sisters,
Always dance
In the direction of holiness.
Always sing
In the direction of heaven.

Our dance is a prayer,
Our song an offering
Of joy and love.

And you will feel
The glory of God's presence
Pass through you.
You will feel
The breath of life
Surround you.
Together, we will become a hymn,
Praise that resounds throughout the earth,
Throughout the ages.
Women will dance this dance,
Sing this song,
Pray this prayer.

Come, sisters,
Summon your joy,
Summon your voice,
Summon your heart,
Summon the generations
To this song,
To this dance.

All praise to God Most High,
Who leads us through moments
Of sorrow and pain,
Of hope and comfort,
Of celebration and victory,
Of triumph and exultation.

Dance, sisters.
Dance.

Offerings

When God offers love, we offer our hearts.
When God offers wisdom, we offer our minds.

When God offers beauty, we offer our senses.
When God offers silence, we offer our patience.

When God offers challenge, we offer our strength.
When God offers trial, we offer our faith.

When God offers pain, we offer our dignity.
When God offers fear, we offer our courage.

When God offers grief, we offer our endurance.
When God offers shame, we offer our amends.

When God offers death, we offer our mourning.
When God offers life, we offer our rejoicing.

When God offers joy, we offer our thanksgiving.
When God offers awe, we offer our wonder.

When God offers righteousness, we offer our blessings.
When God offers holiness, we offer our praise.

Blessed are You, God of gifts, God of blessings,
You fill our lives with meaning.

Umbrella of Blessings

God of mystery,
God of wonder,
Your word is an umbrella of blessing,
Your wisdom a canopy of holiness and light,
A shelter of awe and wonder.

Ancient One,
Your blessings protect the strong
And lift the humble,
Guard the joyous
And support grieving,
Guide the hopeful
And raise the downcast.

Your tent is the arch of the heavens.
Your drape is the firmament of sky.
Your blessings quench our thirst,
Feed the land,
Fill our hearts,
Bring hope and healing.

Blessed are You, Ancient One,
You cover our lives with an umbrella of blessings,
Filling our days with joy and thanksgiving.

Amidah
Standing Prayers

❦

For Devotion

God, open my lips so that my mouth may declare
    Your praise.
Open my mouth, so that my heart may sing
    Your glory.
Open my heart, so that my eyes may see
    Your wisdom.
Open my eyes, so that my soul feels
    Your Presence.
Open my soul, so that my hands do
    Your mitzvot.
Open my hands, so that my works glorify
    Your Torah.
Open my works, so that my deeds bear witness to
    Your truth.
Open my deeds, so that my life bears witness to
    Your justice.
Open my life, so that my spirit bears witness to
    Your mercy.
Open my spirit, so that my days declare
    Your holy name.

Amidah

Open my lips, and I will praise You.
You are our loving God, the God of our ancestors.
You set the journey of the soul and the cycle of nature.
You are sacred, Your name is holy,
Endowing us with intelligence,
Calling us back to you, repentant,
Forgiving us,
Redeeming us,
Healing us,
Regenerating resources,
Ingathering our communities,
Reinstating justice,
Subverting antagonists,
Rewarding the righteous,
Rebuilding Jerusalem,
Revitalizing us with redemption.
Hear this prayer.
Restore Your presence among us.
For our lives and our souls, we thank You.
Bless us, and establish everlasting peace throughout
    the world.

May my words, and my heart's longings
Fit Your desires for me, Adonai,
My Rock and Redeemer.

Avot v'Imahot

Blessed are You,
Adonai our God,
God of generations,
God of our fathers and mothers,
Of Abraham, Isaac, and Jacob,
Of Sarah, Rebekah, Rachel, and Leah.
We know You as the One
Who revealed Yourself to them,
Revealing Your glory and majesty,
Your wisdom and power,
Bestowing blessings in love.
And You know us as the children
Of their children's children.

Blessed are You,
The Shield of our ancestors,
The Rock of generations.

To Do Your Will

God who made Abraham and Sarah,
Moses and Miriam,
God who made scholars and leaders,
The wise and the heroic,
What is my place and my purpose?
What is Your will as I stand ready,
In awe of Your radiance and light?

God whose voice echoes through time,
Whose blessings flow through our lives,
What is my role and my requirement?
How shall I serve Your glorious and holy name?

This is my longing and my desire:
To do Your will in humility and love.
To hear and to teach.
To see and to bless.
To hold and to honor.
To witness and to wonder.

God of generations,
Source of holiness and purpose,
Reveal the mystery of my life,
Open the gates of my heart,
And fill the well of my being
With vigor and delight.
Then my life will stand in tribute to divine justice
    and mercy,
To the wonder of Creation,
To the honor and dedication of our people.

Blessed is the One, Source of truth,
Who reveals meaning and purpose in our daily lives.

Messengers

God of awe and wonder,
Your messengers are all around,
Leading us on Your path,
Guiding us to joy and love.
Open my eyes to the teachers in our midst,
Leading us to Torah and *chesed*,
Righteousness and charity,
With their kindness and their gentle deeds.
Open my heart to know and to understand their ways,
Their joy in service to You
Through their service to others,
So that I may become
A source of Your blessings.

Holy One,
Well of mercy,
Praise to You in heaven and on earth.
Praise for Your messengers among us.
Praise for the Sabbath of our days.
Praise for the Sabbath of our hearts.

Blessed are You, Rock of generations,
Source of all being,
You plant the seeds
Of holiness among us.

Holy

Holiness surrounds me,
Fills the empty space.
Wondrous luminosity,
Radiance and grace.
Pulsing, pulsing,
Heavenly embrace.
Pulsing, pulsing,
To this human place.

The Artist and the canvas,
The Sculptor and the stone,
The Composer and the notepad,
The Potter's clay is thrown.
Creating foundation.
Creating sky and earth.
Vast and small.
Present,
Yearning to be known.

Holiness is waiting,
Here and now and strong.
Waiting for a witness,
A Hallelujah song.

Painted by Your light,
Sculpted, drafted, formed.
Story, dance, and music,
Miracles performed.

My heart will be Your vessel,
A vessel for this light.
Collecting sparks and glimmers,
A marvelous delight.

Holiness is waiting,
Here and now and strong.
Waiting for a witness,
A Hallelujah song.

Without a Sound

I whispered a secret prayer to God,
Who whispered a secret answer to me,
So quietly
That it arrived
In the chambers of my soul
Without a sound.

Oh how I wish to hear Your voice.
Oh how I wish to know Your dreams for me.
Oh how I wish to let my heart run wild and free,
As light as a bird song,
As true as the call of the shofar,
As certain as an angel calling out holy, holy, holy . . .

I whispered a secret prayer to God,
Who whispered a secret answer to me,
To trust
That blessings arrive
In the chambers of my soul
Without a sound.

Let Us Meet

How can You hear me,
God of Old,
How can You hear my voice,
In the chorus of
Song and praise
Reaching toward heaven?

How can I hear You,
God of Old,
How can I hear Your voice,
In the chorus of
Traffic and regret
Weighing on my heart?

Let us meet in the hills at daybreak.
Let us meet in my eyes at sunset.
Let us meet in my labor at noontide.
Let us meet in this yearning at twilight.

My life is a prayer.
Your whispers, a blessing.

Let us meet in sacred moments of holiness and love.
Let us meet in gentle moments of awe and wonder.
Your radiance shimmers across Creation.
My words approach You, a song of delight.

Holy One,
Let us meet
In a heartbeat,
In a breath,
In a vision
Of Your holy mountain,
Where Your word,
Where Your righteousness,
Where Your justice and Your mercy
Bless and sustain
Us all.

The Dark Corners

Fear lurks
In the dark corners of my heart,
Waiting to convince me
That love will fail.

Sorrow lurks
In the dark corners of my soul,
Waiting to convince me
That faith will fail.

Doubt lurks
In the dark corners of my mind,
Waiting to convince me
That wisdom will fail.

Rock of Jacob,
Teach me to shine
The light of mitzvot
Into the dark corners of my mind,
So that I face my fears with courage,
Redeeming them with awe and wonder.

Song of Miriam,
Teach me to shine
The light of *t'filot*
Into the dark corners of my soul,
So that I face my sorrows with strength,
Redeeming them with righteousness.

God of Old,
Teach me to shine
The light of Torah
Into the dark corners of my mind,
So that I face my doubts with honor,
Redeeming them with holiness.

For Healing

God of love,
Cast the light of health and well-being on _____ [*name*],
And all who are ill, injured, infirm, or insecure,
All those who yearn for Your healing hand.
Bless them with healing of body,
Healing of soul,
And healing of spirit.
Grant all in need a full and complete recovery.

Blessed are You, Adonai our God, Source of life.

Release Me

Holy One,
Release me from judgment.
Release me from doubt.
Release me from hunger.
Release me from want.
Release me from loneliness.
Release me from despair.
Release me from disappointment.
Release me from anger and shame.
Release me with Your gentle hand
And a song of hope.
Release me with the light of Your word
And the echo of Your voice.

God of Old,
Guide me to wisdom and strength.
Teach me to break free of the chains
That I have wrapped around my own heart.
Teach me to live a life of service to others,
A life in celebration of Your gifts.
Teach me to see myself through Your loving eyes,
So that I may return, rejoicing,
To You
And Your people.

Redeeming My Life

A part of me
Refuses to forgive
Myself
For my errors, my mistakes,
My oversights and misdeeds.
How can I redeem my life from within
This place of judgment,
Of harsh words and
Somber requirement?

God of Old,
God of justice and truth,
Teach me to restore my life
Through acts of love and kindness,
Thoughtfulness and care,
In support of my
Family and community.
Teach me to surrender my days
To the joy of service to others,
The joy of concern for this world
And generations to come.

Heavenly Guide,
Revive me with Your light,
Restore me with Your truth,
Refresh me with deeds
Of righteousness and charity.

Let Me

Let me be the one
Who reminds you
That wisdom and beauty
Shine through your eyes.

Let me be the one
Who reminds you
That power and courage
Are in your hands and in your heart.

Let me be the one
Who reminds you
That today is your day
To choose righteousness and love.

You are a gift of light.
You are a well of strength.
You are a message of hope

Let me be the one
Who reminds you
To sing, to pray,
To dance, to bless,
To feed the hungry,
To clothe the naked,
To free the captive,
To redeem the oppressed.
And you will remind me
To be the man/woman our God intended.
Then, together, we will be messengers
Of Torah and truth,
Bringing holiness into the world.

Blessed are You, God of all,
You call on us to use our gifts
To heal the world.

Quiet

In the quiet,
My breath is the wind,
My heartbeat is thunder.

In the quiet,
My spirit settles,
And my soul rests.

In the quiet,
All that I am,
Meets everyone I might be.

God,
Grant me moments of gentleness,
Moments of gratitude,
Moments of calm,
Moments of peace,
So that I might hear the echoes of eternity,
And the stillness within,
So that I might live a life
Of joy and laughter,
Wisdom and dignity,
Love and honor,
In service to myself,
In service to others,
In service to Your holy name.

Blessed are the gentle
Moments of grace.

On Making a Mistake

God of realms above and realms below,
Of justice and mercy,
Grant me the understanding that my mistakes
Are teachers and guides,
Pointing me in the direction of my best self,
Leading me toward a path of righteousness,
A path of charity,
A path of love.

Redeemer of Israel,
Bless my mistakes with the power to teach.
Remove the potential for harm.
Give me the strength and wisdom to amend my ways,
To seek forgiveness and live by my ideals
Guided by Your word.

Blessed are You, who reveals the path of righteousness.

Sin Offering

I stand before You this day
God of Old,
To offer my sins
As tribute to my humanity,
To offer my repentance
As tribute to my holiness.
Teach me to cast off these sins,
To make space for Your radiance and light,
To make space for my humanity and this holiness
To meet in the core of my being,
So that my soul may shine brighter,
So that the works of my hands
Will praise Your Creation,
So that my life will be a blessing
In heaven and on earth.

For Jewish Unity

May it be Your will,
Adonai our God,
God of our mothers and fathers,
To restore the Jewish people to each other
In wholeness and love.
May our differences in understanding and practice
Never be a source of *sinat chinam*, *chas v'shalom*,
Nor physical violence, *chas v'shalom*.
May our love for Torah and each other shine forth
From Jerusalem to the four corners of the earth,
Speedily, in our days.

Against Hatred

For those who hate,
Let there be no hope,
And may all derision and disdain perish in an instant.
May intolerance be swiftly cut down.
May You quickly uproot, crush, cast down, and humble
    the arrogant,
Speedily in our days.
Blessed are You, Adonai,
Who destroys enemies and humbles the arrogant.

To Hear Your Voice

Divine voice of reason and love,
Of compassion and understanding:
 Speak gently and clearly so that I may know Your will.
 Give me the patience to listen and the desire to seek
 Your counsel and instruction.
 Grant me the understanding to hear Your teachings
  in every voice,
 From all people,
 In every moment of need.
Open my heart to others,
To their suffering,
To their call for help.
Open my heart to love and laughter,
Song and dance,
Beauty and grace,
So that I remember to celebrate Your gifts day by day.

 Divine Creator of spirit and light,
 Teach me to hold my joys and sorrows gently in my hands
 And to honor them both.
 Teach me to be present to all that I see and all that I feel,
 In truth, without fear.
 Teach me to be present for others
 In humble service.

Blessed are You,
Teacher and Guide,
You make Your wisdom known to those who ask
And those who listen, willingly and patiently,
To the voices of Your Creation.

Blessed are You, Your voice resounds throughout Creation.

To Seek Your Glory

Divine Author of Creation,
Well of mystery,
Majestic hand of light and truth,
Grant me the patience and wisdom
To seek Your wonders,
The glory of Your sacred and holy name.
Open my eyes to radiance and splendor,
The steady flow of holiness and love,
To awe, abundance, beauty, comfort, and rest.
Set us on the path of devotion and dedication,
A wondrous journey of discovery.
Give us energy, endurance, and enthusiasm,
Zest and zeal,
To live our lives in wonder,
Seeking Your holy presence.

God of all being,
Font of wisdom and joy,
Your glory endures.

To Know Your Word

Divine teacher,
Source of knowledge, wisdom, and insight,
Well of secrets,
Creation sings your praise.
Sea, earth, and sky proclaim your majesty.
Your word resounds around us,
And Your voice echoes throughout the universe.

God of ancient secrets,
Holy One of Old,
Open my heart to Your guidance
And my mind to Your teaching,
So that I may know Your word
And live by Your holy command,
So that I may be of service to You,
Your people,
And Your Torah.

Blessed are You, Rock of truth,
Your word resounds from the heavens,
Your teachings fill the earth.

To Seek Your Love

Divine Creator of beauty and light,
In wisdom You wait,
In love You hope,
In service You pray.
You pray for us to seek the radiance and splendor
Of the seen and unseen glories hidden in Your Creation.
You pray for us to yearn for You,
As You yearn for us.

Holy One,
Ancient One,
Rock of life,
Let my thirst for You lead me on a righteous path,
On a path of joy and surrender,
A path of generous love.
Make me a witness to the constant flow of divine gifts,
So that I remember to seek You in joy.

Blessed are You, Adonai, delighting in Your people's love.

For Grace

All I am,
All I have,
All I'll become,
Are present in this moment:
Warmth and breath,
Love and compassion,
Silence and celebration.
Everything, here.
All gifts, present.

What then, God of all being,
What then of my choices?
What will I make of the space
Between this breath and the next?
Will I bring laughter and light,
Hope and faith,
Wonder and strength?
Will I stand in humble service
For all of my brothers and sisters?

Maker of heaven and earth,
Grant us the wisdom to choose lives of grace,
Of vision and understanding,
Seeing each moment as a choice
To bless our companions
With strength and wisdom,
With honor and respect.

Blessed are the gentle moments of grace.

For Wonder and Awe

My body is Yours, O my God,
My limbs Your tools, my heart Your dwelling.
Open my heart to receive Your gifts,
Wonder and awe,
Grace and majesty,
Full yet humble,
A symphony of song and delight.

As for me,
I have chased dust in vain pursuit,
Pursued shadows in selfish desire,
Grasped for wind instead of seeking You,
My Rock,
My Holy Shelter.

My body is Yours, O my God,
My life abundant,
My moments bursting with love.
Give me new wisdom,
To live by Your word,
To honor Your holy name,
So that Your gifts to me
Return to You as blessings.

Prayer with Wings

Just once, Holy One,
Just once before I die
Let me feel my prayers with my entire being,
The radiance and the glory of my heart
Rising to meet You,
My soul reaching toward the unreachable,
My eyes blazing toward the unseeable,
My mind open to the unknowable,
My blood flowing gracefully through Your river of light.
Let me become a prayer with wings,
Gliding on the currents of faith,
Soaring into beams from heaven
Bursting forth from the moment of Creation.

Just once, Holy One,
Just once before I die
Let my prayers enter the gates of heaven,
To plead for peace and
To sing Your praise.

Prayer of Gratitude

Today is a gift,
O my God,
To know Your world,
To receive Your blessings.

Rock of Ages,
Your works surround us,
Daily signs of awe and wonder,
Daily guides to joy and service.
Bless me with hands of strength,
A heart of courage,
A mind of understanding.
Bless me with a voice of praise,
A life of gratitude,
Days filled with hope and love.

We Are Music

Quiet now.
Listen.
Breathe.
And listen.

You are music.
Your breath and hands,
Your smile and tears,
Your eyes and pulse,
Are notes that dance
In the space between us.

We are music.
A symphony conducted
By the rhythm of life,
By God's hand,
By our choices, day by day.

Our notes play on,
Separately, together,
The sacred sound of living.
Our music waltzes,
Making melodies fresh and new,
Never heard again,
Bass lines that pulse from our hearts
To the Soul of the universe.

Joy bends sorrow.
Sorrow bends hope.
Hope bends grief.
Grief bends love.
Love bends joy.

Quiet now.
Listen.
Breathe.
And listen.

The silence is your longing.
The silence is your yearning for a different song.
The music of your own will
Blocks your heart to the harmonies
Already dancing around you,
To the chorus already singing around you.

Oh, you hidden delight of heaven.
Oh, you secret gift of God.
We are music.
We are music.
The music plays through us.

Marvelous Gifts

God of Old,
We give thanks
For moments of wonder and awe,
Of righteousness and charity,
For the freedom to do Your will.
Let Your mysteries unfold around us.
Guide us,
Shield us,
Lift us from narrow places
Of fear and despair
Into lives of service,
Into lives of celebration.
Teach me to use my hours with care
And my words as tools of praise.

The world is beautiful,
Marvelous in opportunity,
Joyous in energy,
Pulsing with excitement,
Vibrant in youth,
Wise in years,
Amazing with vitality,
Fantastic in all life,
A place of love and hope.
Teach me to use my hands to build,
And my heart as a beacon of joy.

God of all being,
Let me use the gift of redemption
From slavery to freedom,
From despair to hope,
As an instrument of holiness,
Celebrating the glory and beauty of Creation,
A remembrance of our Exodus from Egypt.

Peace Will Come

Peace will come,
Through the grace of God
And the work of humanity:
Compassion and kindness,
Forgiveness and love,
Patience and gratitude,
Justice and mercy,
Empathy and understanding,
Each act a yearning,
Each deed a longing,
For wholeness and tranquility
In our world.

You who makes peace in the highest heavens,
Guide our hearts and our hands
In service to each other and Your world,
To bring peace to all the nations of the earth,
All people, everywhere.

Seder K'riat HaTorah
Torah Service

God's Voice

What if God's voice was so near
That your bones rattled
As thunder echoes inside your chest?

What if God's voice was so near
You could feel the wind hit your face
As your feet seem to slip on shaking ground?

What if awe and wonder surrounded you,
So close that your knees buckled,
As a pillar of fire from heaven descends to earth?

What if holiness packed the empty space with light
As your lungs fill with the one divine breath
Together with every other living being?

What if God's voice is as near
As your willingness to remember
The moment we stood together at Sinai,
Amid the smoke and the lightning,
Hearing the great blast of the shofar?

What if that moment
Is now?

Let Torah

Let Torah hold your moments,
Carry your days,
Lift your years.

Let Torah fill your hands,
Nourish your breath,
Refresh your heart.

Let Torah sustain your words,
Enliven your deeds,
Lead you home.

For Torah is in each life and each generation,
In the yearning for God and in God's yearning for us,
The flow of secrets from Sinai,
In divine guidance and grace,
Calling out to you, dear sisters and brothers:
   "Awake, you slumberers!
    Awake, you who wander empty and lonely without
      wonder and awe.
    Have you forgotten this precious gift?
    Have you forsaken your past and your future?
    Have you traded your birthright for empty promises?"

This, then, is God's command:
Let Torah hold you,
Fill you,
Sustain you.
Let Torah guide you into radiance and mystery.
Study and learn,
Question and seek,
Hear and grow,
Lifting your life in sacred service.
Let Torah be your breath and your heartbeat.

Blessed are You, Source of Torah.

Ki MiTzion

Let Torah pour forth
From Jerusalem and Zion.
Let Torah pour forth
From our hearts and our hands.
Let Torah pour forth
From our words and our deeds.
Torah is our light and our salvation.
Torah is our protection and our hope.
And God will be with us,
And God will bless us,
As Torah lights our way.

כִּי מִצִּיוֹן תֵּצֵא תוֹרָה,
וּדְבַר יי מִירוּשָׁלֵָיִם.

Ki miTzion teitzei Torah,
Ud'var Adonai miY'rushalayim.
For from out of Zion will come the Torah,
And the word of Adonai from Jerusalem.

Prayers for Healing

Bring Healing Power

God, grant Your healing power
To all in need,
Those whom I know,
And those unknown to me.

God, grant Your comfort and consolation
To all who grieve,
Those whom I know,
And those unknown to me.

Holy One,
Bring a swift end to suffering and strife,
And heal the world
With Your steadfast love.

Living Waters

Let the well of living waters
Flow through me
From the Source,
From ancient pools
Of holiness and light,
Ancient pools that sustain the body
And soothe the heart.

My grief has turned
My heart to stone,
My sorrow and loneliness
Have hardened my veins.
Crack me open with Your divine rod.
Release my tears with Your staff.
Let me know wholeness
And peace,
Once again.

R'fuat HaNefesh

God of the spirit,
God of the soul, the breath, and the wind,
Look with kindness and favor on
_____ [names],
Whose hearts ache,
Crushed and fallow,
Whose hearts yearn,
Empty and broken.
God of the *nefesh*, *ruach*, and *n'shamah*,
Guide these souls
Back to wonder and mystery,
Sacred moments and glorious days,
So that they know the power of Your love
And the wisdom of Your word.
May their souls shine,
A light and blessing
For our people Israel.

Tears

The mothers of Israel
Pass their tears
From generation to generation:
The grief and the longing,
Hope and surrender,
The breathless yearning,
Gifted mother to daughter
For millennia.

Daughters of Israel,
Your tears are a prayer,
An offering on the altar of our lives,
Rising to the gates of righteousness,
Summoning Sarah and Miriam,
Leah and Rachel,
Rebekah and Dinah,
Hannah and Penina,
Deborah and Yael,
Esther and Tamar,
Naomi and Ruth,
The midwives of Egypt and the daughters of Zelophehad,
Matriarchs and prophets, leaders and teachers,
The entire tent of women throughout the ages

To cry out:
> Heal us, God of old.
> Shelter us, God of love.
> Make us whole.

Sisters of Israel,
You are our light.
You are our heartbeat.
Your sorrows are our plea
Before the gates of mercy.
Lead us into prayer.
Lead us from darkness to light.
Lead us in service to God's holy name.

Being a Blessing

If you ask for rest, I will sit with you.
If you ask for comfort, I will stay with you.

If you ask for hope, I will yearn with you.
If you ask for love, I will sing with you.

If you ask for stillness, I will breathe with you.
If you ask for peace, I will dream with you.

If you ask for joy, I will laugh with you.
If you ask for healing, I will pray with you.

If you ask for warmth, I will become a blanket.
If you ask for refuge, I will become a shelter.

If you ask for help, I will become a blessing.

For Our Congregation

God of Old,
Bless our holy congregation.
We are Your servants,
Men, women, and children,
Old and young,
Lovers of Torah,
The strong and the infirm,
Teachers and students,
Lovers of Your way.

God whose name is Mercy,
God whose name is Truth,
Our lives are in Your hands.
Our time is fleeting.
You number our days.
Grant our congregation steadfast compassion,
Enduring devotion,
Strength, wisdom, and kindness.
Let us celebrate together with fullness of heart.
Let us mourn together under a tent of comfort and care.
Together, we will serve You from generation
    to generation,
A light of hope,
A light of love,
A light of Your Holy Word.

מִי שֶׁבֵּרַךְ אֲבוֹתֵינוּ וְאִמּוֹתֵנוּ,
אַבְרָהָם, יִצְחָק, וְיַעֲקֹב, שָׂרָה, רִבְקָה, רָחֵל וְלֵאָה,
הוּא יְבָרֵךְ אֶת הַקָּהָל הַקָּדוֹשׁ הַזֶּה
לְחַיִּים וּלְשָׁלוֹם,
לְשָׂשׂוֹן וּלְשִׂמְחָה,
לִישׁוּעָה וּלְנֶחָמָה: וְנֹאמַר אָמֵן.

Mi shebeirach avoteinu v'imoteinu,
Avraham, Yitzchak, v'Yaakov,
Sarah, Rivkah, Rachel, v'Lei-ah,
hu y'vareich et
hakahal hakadosh hazeh
l'chayim ul'shalom,
l'sason ul'simchah,
lishuah ul'nechamah: v'nomar Amen.

May the One who blessed our fathers
Abraham, Isaac, and Jacob,
And our mothers
Sarah, Rebekah, Rachel, and Leah,
Bless this holy congregation
With life and peace,
Joy and gladness,
Deliverance and consolation,
And let us say: Amen.

For Congregational Wisdom during Conflict

God of Old,
We come together
As a congregation,
A community of men and women,
Young and old,
In reverence for each other,
With challenges facing us as a community,
And we look for insight and guidance.

We have one desire:
To build a place of holiness,
A place of Torah,
A place of *chesed* and *rachamim*.

Grant us wisdom as we do this holy work.
Grant us the ability to speak with care,
And to listen with understanding.
Open our hearts
So that our words will build deeper connections
And stronger bonds,
In this holy congregation.

מִי שֶׁבֵּרַךְ אֲבוֹתֵינוּ וְאִמּוֹתֵנוּ,
אַבְרָהָם, יִצְחָק, וְיַעֲקֹב, שָׂרָה, רִבְקָה, רָחֵל וְלֵאָה,
הוּא יְבָרֵךְ אֶת הַקָּהָל הַקָּדוֹשׁ הַזֶּה
לְחַיִּים וּלְשָׁלוֹם,
לְשָׂשׂוֹן וּלְשִׂמְחָה,
לִישׁוּעָה וּלְנֶחָמָה: וְנֹאמַר אָמֵן.

Mi shebeirach avoteinu v'imoteinu,
Avraham, Yitzchak, v'Yaakov,
Sarah, Rivkah, Rachel, v'Lei-ah,
hu y'vareich et
hakahal hakadosh hazeh
l'chayim ul'shalom,
l'sason ul'simchah,
lishuah ul'nechamah: v'nomar Amen.

May the one who blessed our fathers
Abraham, Isaac, and Jacob,
And our mothers
Sarah, Rebekah, Rachel, and Leah,
Bless this holy congregation
With life and peace,
Joy and gladness,
Deliverance and consolation,
And let us say: Amen.

For Government

יְקוּם פֻּרְקָן מִן שְׁמַיָּא
Yikum purkan min sh'maya
Let deliverance arise from heaven
Bringing justice and enlightenment
To the nations of the earth
And to the leaders of our nation,

חִנָּא וְחִסְדָּא וְרַחֲמֵי
China v'chisda v'rachamei
Bringing grace, love, and compassion
To the halls of power,
The seats of government,
The capitals of our world.

הַנּוֹתֵן תְּשׁוּעָה וּמֶמְשָׁלָה לַנְּסִיכִים
HaNotein t'shuah u'memshalah lan'sichim
You who give redemption and governance to presidents,
Reward us with political leaders
With true vision and deep understanding
Of Your instructions to rebuild
And renew the earth,
So that economic, legal,
Social, and environmental justice
May bear fruit
For generations to come.

יְהִי רָצוֹן מִלְפָנֶיךָ
Y'hi ratzon milfanecha
May it be Your will
To grant the heads of state
A new vision
For safety and prosperity,
Friendship and cooperation,

So that all may know
The fullness of Your blessings,
In a world of generosity and kindness,
Tranquility and peace.

הַנּוֹתֵן תְּשׁוּעָה וּמֶמְשָׁלָה לַנְּסִיכִים
HaNotein t'shuah u'memshalah lan'sichim
May You who reward redemption and governance
    to presidents,
Reward us with political leaders
With true vision and deep understanding
Of Your instructions to rebuild
And renew the earth,
So that economic, legal,
Social, and environmental justice
May bear fruit
For generations to come.

For Wisdom during Democratic Elections

God of justice,
Protector and Redeemer,
Grant guidance to our nation
As we select leaders
To serve and to govern,
The men and women who promise
To bring prosperity to our land,
The men and women who promise
To protect our homes and secure our borders.

Grant wisdom and courage to voters
To entrust our government to visionaries and leaderss,
To those who will serve our citizens,
And all who reside within our borders,
With honor and integrity
To forge a flourishing and peaceful future.

Bless our [president/prime minister] and
The [Congress/Parliament/Knesset/legislature]
With vision and strength,
Fortitude and insight.
May they lead us to a time
When liberty and equality will
Reign supreme throughout the land.

God of truth,
Source and Shelter,
Grant safety and security to all nations,
So that truth and harmony will resound
From the four corners of the earth.
Let the light of [this/our/the U.S./the Israeli/
    the (country name)] democracy
Shine brightly,
A beacon of hope
For every land and every people.

For Peace in the Middle East

Sons of Abraham,
Sons of Hagar and Sarah,
Of Isaac and Ishmael:
Have you forgotten the day we buried our father?
Have you forgotten the day we carried his dead body
     into the cave near Hebron?
Have you forgotten the day we entered the darkness
     of Machpelah to lay our patriarch to rest?

Sons of Esau and Jacob:
Have you forgotten the day we made peace?
The day we set aside past injustices and deep wounds
     to lay down our weapons and live?
Or the day we, too, buried our father together? Have you
     forgotten that we took Isaac's corpse into that humble
     cave to place him with his father for eternity?

Brother, I don't remember crying with you.
Sister, I don't remember mourning with you.
We should have cried the tears of generations.
We should have cried the tears of centuries,
The tears of fatherless sons
And motherless daughters,
So that we would remember in our flesh that we are
     one people,
From one father on earth and one Creator in heaven,
Divided only by time and history.

One God,
My brother calls you Allah.
My sister calls you Adonai.
You speak to some through Moses.
You speak to some through Muhammad.
We are one family, cousins and kin.

Holy One,
Light of truth,
Source of wisdom and strength,
In the name of our fathers and mothers,
In the name of justice and peace,
Help us to remember our history,
To mourn our losses together,
So that we may,
Once more,
Lay down our weapons and live.

God of all being,
Bring peace and justice to the land,
And joy to our hearts.

For Travel

God, who watches over us,
Watch over this journey.
Keep us free from affliction and strife,
Safe from danger and wrongdoing,
Protected in Your loving sight.

May we know strength and good fortune on the way,
Rest and peace upon our return.
May this travel be blessed with the shelter of Your
    gentle arms,
The guidance of Your mighty hand,
The gift of Your countless blessings.

Bless our moments apart,
Bless our moments together.
Grace upon departure,
Joy upon return.
Remembering to praise and bless
Your holy name
Wherever You lead us.

To Ask

Holy One,
God of my heart,
What is it that You ask of me,
In my joy and wonder?
What is it that You ask of me,
In my grief and pain?
What is it that You ask of me,
In my vitality and strength?
What is it that You ask of me,
In my weakness and decline?

Ancient One,
Grant me the will and the desire,
The spirit and the purpose,
To serve You with love,
To ask for Your guidance,
To seek Your help,
To do Your will,
To learn Your Torah,
To act with righteousness,
To live with humility,
To rejoice in all Your gifts.

The Statutes of Heaven

This will be a law,
An ordinance of heaven,
A statute for all time
That I will obey.
Love.
Love so that my hands
Yearn to heal.
Love so that my eyes
Yearn for holiness and beauty.
Love so that sacred words of Torah
Are forever on my lips.
I will do and I will listen.

And if I forget
To love this life I've been given,
If I forget to love the God of my people,
The homeless and the stranger,
The widow and the orphan,
The statutes of heaven will remind me
Against a callous heart,
Against neglect and deceit,
Against contempt and vain pursuit.

These are the first fruits of my heart.
Kindness and charity.
Thanksgiving and mourning.
Joy and sorrow.
Repentance and prayer.
Honor, wisdom, and grace.
I will not withhold them
From my God,
Neither the fullness of my being,
Nor the richness of my celebration.

The statutes of heaven are my guide.
They resound from Sinai into my life.
This will be a law,
An ordinance of heaven,
A statute for all time.
Love through service,
Love through Torah and mitzvot,
Love through a life of holiness.

Tree of Life

Torah of life,
Resounding with wisdom,
Everlasting joy,
Everlasting righteousness,

Of your beauty and mystery,
Forever we sing.

Lift up our hearts,
In hope and faith,
For this is the path of pleasantness,
Everlasting peace.

Concluding Prayers

Every Heart

Let us exalt
Your holy name,
Proclaiming Your majesty,
Proclaiming Your sovereignty,
Proclaiming Your splendor.
Let our limbs announce Your radiance,
And our voices declare Your glory.
Let us sing and shout,
So that the hills echo with praise
And the streets pulse with prayer,
So that the seas swell with rejoicing
And the cities vibrate with thanksgiving.
Then the universe will expand with wonder,
And the heavenly host will join in the song.
The gates of righteousness will burst open.
The path to mystery will shine.
The way to holiness will sparkle.
The route to beauty will gleam.
Every heart will turn to You,
Adonai our God,
In joyous surrender.
Every heart will know gratitude and love,
Happiness and consolation.
Justice and mercy will reign,
And peace will hallow the earth.

The Open Space

Wholeness is the open space,
The place between,
Where the rhythm of being
Enters, flows through,
In my vision and my courage.

Forgiveness is the open space
Where yesterday meets tomorrow,
Where the tide waits to shift,
Where holiness blesses the mundane,
In my breath and my celebration.

Wisdom is the open space
Where the echo hears the wind,
Where the silence becomes God's voice,
Where all that I am meets all that I can be,
In my marrow and in my surrender.

One Gift

There is but one gift
That is the source of all blessings:
The gift of now.
Now is the source
Of you, my friend,
Of us, my love,
Of sky and rain,
Of thunder and light,
Of season and harvest,
Of mystery and adventure,
Of awe and wonder.
Now is the source of blessings.

There is but one Source
For this well of blessings,
This flow of now:
You, God of all being.
You are the Source
Of friendship and love,
Of tide and bounty,
Of endings and beginnings,
Of Torah and wisdom,
Of radiance and splendor,
Of holiness and healing.
You, Holy One, are the
Source of all gifts, the
Source of all blessings, the
Source of now.

For the Bereaved

Rock of Jacob,
Comfort of Rachel,
Broken and torn,
Shattered and crushed,
Bereaved and bereft,
We declare Your holy name.

We praise Your gifts and Your works.
You are Author and Artist,
Architect and Builder,
Source and Redeemer.

We, the mourners of Zion and Israel,
Comfort each other.
We console the lonely and embrace the lost.
We cry each other's tears.
Together we recall Your wonder and Your majesty.

Holy One,
Ineffable Redeemer,
Guiding Hand,
Gentle Hand,
Loving Hand,
Light of Israel,
You are our Shelter.

Every Beginning

Every beginning brings an ending.
Every ending brings a beginning.

Ancient One,
This is the joy and the grief,
The plenty and the famine,
The dance and the dirge
Of life,
Alive and awake
In Your world.

How wonderful is this living?
How glorious the light from heaven?
How stunning the radiance that surrounds you,
My beloved,
Holy and new, luminous with wonder?
How marvelous this place where earth and sky touch?

How strange is this dying?
How melancholy that one day we will
No longer hear sweet voices,
See sweet faces,
Share whispers and secrets,
Laughter and heartbreak?
How much more
Should we love today?
How much more, my children,
Should we savor and rejoice?

Every beginning brings an ending.
Every ending brings a beginning.

Blessed is God's holy name.

The Last Moment

What if this is the last moment
Of Creation?
The last moment we have to share
Our joy, our hope, our love.

What if this is the last moment
With you on earth?
The last to chance feel
Your breath, your heart, your surrender.
When you depart,
The world will remain,
Full of mystery and wonder.

What if this is the last moment
With me on earth?
The last chance to offer
My hand, my smile, my strength.
When I depart,
The world will remain,
Full of glory and holiness.

What if this is the last moment
We have together?
The only chance we have to share
Our awe, our power, our peace.
When we say goodbye,
The world will remain.
The sky will continue to fill with radiance.
The core of the earth will still burn
Molten hot with passion for living.
And light, light from the edge of the universe,
Light from the day when God spoke
And the world came to be,
Will reach my face
And will warm your heart.

Soul Shine

Let your soul shine
In your chest.
Let your heart sparkle
In your eyes.
Let joy
Fill your limbs with radiance.
Let love
Fill your hands with splendor.
You are the instrument
Of God's music,
The tool
Of repairing the earth.
You are the voice
Of wonder and awe,
The song
Of hope and tomorrow.

This gift,
This majesty within,
Is not yours to keep.
It is not yours to hold.
It is not yours to hide.

Let your soul shine
Luminous, elegant,
Brave and true,
A beacon of praise,
A lantern of song,
A summons for holiness
To enter our lives
And this world.

Let your soul shine.
Set it free.
Set it free to fill the space
Between the here
And the unknown
With abundance
And with blessings.

Whispered Prayer

Your whispered prayer,
Your secret hope,
Your quiet yearning,
Have holiness and power.
They resound in the heavens
And echo on high.
They are drum and cymbal,
Trumpet and horn,
Proclaiming your faith,
Music of generations,
Proclaiming your hope,
Hymns of the heart,
Proclaiming your dedication
To the God of all being,
Source and Shelter,
Rock and Redeemer,
Light and Truth.

Your whispered prayer
Is the song of the ages.
Your secret hope
Is the light of tomorrow.
Your quiet yearning
Is the voice of eternity.

Blessed are You,
Adonai our God,
Who hears prayer.

בָּרוּךְ אַתָּה, יי, שׁוֹמֵעַ תְּפִלָּה.
Baruch atah, Adonai, shomei-a t'filah.

Let Tranquility Reign

Some days,
Ancient One,
Some days the prayers
Of Your people
Are so close
We can hold them in our hands,
Feel them with our eyes,
Taste them with our breath.
They surround our hearts
To become our yearning.
They surround our song
To become our grieving.
They surround our souls
To become our pleading.

"My soul has dwelled too long
Among those who hate peace.
I am for peace, but when I speak of it
They are for war."

רַבַּת שָׁכְנָה לָהּ נַפְשִׁי עִם שׂוֹנֵא שָׁלוֹם.
אֲנִי שָׁלוֹם וְכִי אֲדַבֵּר הֵמָּה לַמִּלְחָמָה.

Rabat shachnah lah nafshi im sonei shalom.
Ani shalom v'chi adabeir heimah lamil'chamah.

When will peace come,
Source of peace,
When will sorrow be vanquished?
When will tranquility reign?

"Adonai will guard you from all harm;
God will guard your soul.
Adonai will guard your going and coming;
Now and evermore."

יי יִשְׁמָרְךָ מִכָּל־רָע, יִשְׁמֹר אֶת־נַפְשֶׁךָ.
יי יִשְׁמָר־צֵאתְךָ וּבוֹאֶךָ, מֵעַתָּה וְעַד־עוֹלָם.

Adonai yishmarcha mikol ra, yishmor et nafshecha.
Adonai yishmor tzeit'cha uvo-echa, mei-atah v'ad olam.

For You are our hope.
Our comfort.
Our blessing.
Let those who cherish life
Bless this day and every day.

"For the sake of my comrades and companions,
I shall say: 'Peace be within you.'
For the sake of the House of Adonai our God,
I will seek your good."

לְמַעַן אַחַי וְרֵעָי, אֲדַבְּרָה־נָּא שָׁלוֹם בָּךְ.
לְמַעַן בֵּית־יי אֱלֹהֵינוּ אֲבַקְשָׁה טוֹב לָךְ.

L'maan achai v'rei-ai adab'rah na shalom bach.
L'maan beit Adonai Eloheinu avak'shah tov lach.

Let these prayers ascend
To the lofty heights,
So that the nations
And peoples of the earth
Will rejoice in holiness,
Will rejoice in splendor,
And will rejoice, together, in righteousness.

Biographies

ALDEN SOLOVY is a liturgist, author, journalist, and teacher. He's written more than seven hundred pieces of new liturgy, offering a fresh new Jewish voice, challenging the boundaries between poetry, meditation, personal growth, and prayer. His writing was transformed by multiple tragedies, marked in 2009 by the sudden death of his wife from catastrophic brain injury. Solovy's teaching spans from Hebrew Union College–Jewish Institute of Religion in Jerusalem, to Limmud in the United Kingdom, and as a liturgist/scholar-in-residence at synagogues throughout North America. The *Jerusalem Post* called his writing "soulful, meticulously crafted." *Huffington Post Religion* said, "The prayers reflect age-old yearnings in modern-day situations." Solovy is a three-time winner of the Peter Lisagor Award for Exemplary Journalism. He made *aliyah* to Israel in 2012, where he hikes, writes, teaches, and learns. His work has appeared in these CCAR Press editions: *Mishkan R'fuah: Where Healing Resides* (2012), *L'chol Z'man v'Eit: For Sacred Moments* (2015), *Mishkan HaNefesh: Machzor for the Days of Awe* (2015), and *Gates of Shabbat,* Revised Edition (2016). He latest works are posted weekly to www.tobendlight.com.

SALLY J. PRIESAND, America's first female rabbi, was ordained in 1972, by Hebrew Union College-Jewish Institute of Religion in Cincinnati, Ohio. From 1981 to 2006, she served as Rabbi of Monmouth Reform

Temple in Tinton Falls, NJ, becoming Rabbi Emerita upon her retirement. She now spends her time traveling the country, accepting invitations to speak about her career and tell the story of Rabbi Regina Jonas. She also participates actively in various organizations in her community serving as President of Interfaith Neighbors, an organization whose primary purpose is to provide rental assistance and support services for the working poor. A native of Cleveland, Ohio, Rabbi Priesand lives in Ocean Township, New Jersey, with her Boston Terrier Zeke. She is a contributor to many books, the most recent of which is *The Sacred Calling: Four Decades of Women in the Rabbinate*, a winner of the National Jewish Book Award.

Permissions

The following are reprinted with permission from *This Grateful Heart: Psalms and Prayers for a New Day* (CCAR Press, 2017): "For Creation"; "Morning Blessings"; "Affirmation of Faith"; "Modeh/Modah Ani"; and "God's Voice." The following are reprinted with permission from *Haggadah Companion: Meditations and Readings* (Kavanot Press, 2014): "Release Me"; "Redeeming My Life"; "Sing Praises"; "Marvelous Gifts"; and "Miriam's Word."

The following are reprinted with permission from *Jewish Prayers of Hope and Healing* (Kavanot Press, 2013): "Each Day"; "For the Bereaved"; "R'fuat HaNefesh"; "To Hear Your Voice"; "To Seek Your Love"; "Sing Hallelujah"; "Offerings"; "For Devotion"; "Every Heart"; "Whispered Prayer"; "Sing Out"; "This Moment"; "For Healing"; "Every Beginning"; and "The Open Space."